MILITARY MACHINES

SUBMARINES AND SUBMERSIBLES

By Drew Nelson

Gareth Stevens
Publishing

Please visit our website, www.garethstevens.com. For a free color catalog of all our high-quality books, call toll free 1-800-542-2595 or fax 1-877-542-2596.

Library of Congress Cataloging-in-Publication Data

Nelson, Drew, 1986-
 Submarines and submersibles / Drew Nelson.
    p. cm. — (Military machines)
 Includes index.
 ISBN 978-1-4339-8478-5 (pbk.)
 ISBN 978-1-4339-8479-2 (6-pack)
 ISBN 978-1-4339-8477-8 (library binding)
 1. Submarines (Ships)—Juvenile literature. 2. Submarines (Ships)—History—Juvenile literature. I. Title.
 VM365.N45 2012
 623.825'7—dc23

                              2012023051

First Edition

Published in 2013 by
Gareth Stevens Publishing
111 East 14th Street, Suite 349
New York, NY 10003

Copyright © 2013 Gareth Stevens Publishing

Designer: Michael J. Flynn
Editor: Kristen Rajczak

Photo credits: Courtesy of the US Navy: cover, pp. 1 Chief Photographer's Mate Andrew McKaskle, 18–19, 20 by Ray Narimatsu, 23 by nicole Hawley, 24 by Chief Photographer's Mate Chris Desmond, 25 by Mass Communication Specialist Seaman James Seward, 26 by Photographer's Mate 2nd Class Michael Sandberg, p. 27 by Senior Chief Mass Communication Specialist Andrew McKaskle; p. 5 US Navy/Getty Images; pp. 6, 15 Hulton Archive/Getty Images; p. 7 http://en.wikipedia.org/wiki/File:Drebbel_Van_Sichem_ca_1631_groot. jpg; p. 9 Science & Society Picture Library/Getty Images; pp. 10, 21 Getty Images; p. 11 MPI/Archive Photos/ Getty Images; pp. 12–13 courtesy of the US Naval Historical Center; p. 14 Topical Press Agency/Hulton Archive/Getty Images; p. 17 (top) George Eastman House/Archive Photos/Getty Images; p. 17 (bottom) PhotoQuest/Archive Photos/Getty Images; p. 29 Colin Anderson/Photographer's Choice/Getty Images.

Printed in the United States of America

CPSIA compliance information: Batch #CW13GS: For further information contact Gareth Stevens, New York, New York at 1-800-542-2595.

CONTENTS

Words in the glossary appear in **bold** type the first time they are used in the text.

WHAT ARE SUBMARINES AND SUBMERSIBLES?

Deep under the sea, a crew of brave sailors is on a secret **mission** to find out the position of an enemy's navy. The crew hasn't seen the sky in 3 months, but they stay underwater to move without being seen. They trained for this, knowing that living and working on a submarine can be dangerous.

Submarines and submersibles are two types of military machines. They travel on and under the water to carry out missions. They move people and supplies, and can have weapons for attacks or special gear to keep an eye on enemies.

What's the Difference?

Submarines are usually bigger than submersibles, but there is another difference that separates them. Submarines can run on their own power and produce their own oxygen, while submersibles work with a larger ship, a submarine, or a team on land.

Submarines
use advanced
technology to
do everything
from locking their
doors to diving
underwater.

5

The history of submarines stretches all the way back to 1578! A former member of the British Royal Navy, William Bourne, **designed** a boat that could be **submerged** in water and rowed. It would have a frame made of wood and be covered in waterproof leather.

Bourne's design was never built. But a Dutch doctor named Cornelius Van Drebbel made a similar vessel in England in 1620. It used tubes to supply air to the crew and allow it to stay underwater for hours at a time. It was able to **maneuver** at 12 to 15 feet (3.7 to 4.6 m) below the surface.

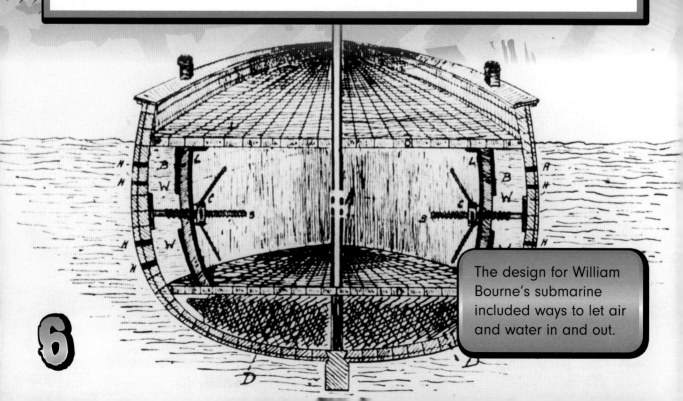

The design for William Bourne's submarine included ways to let air and water in and out.

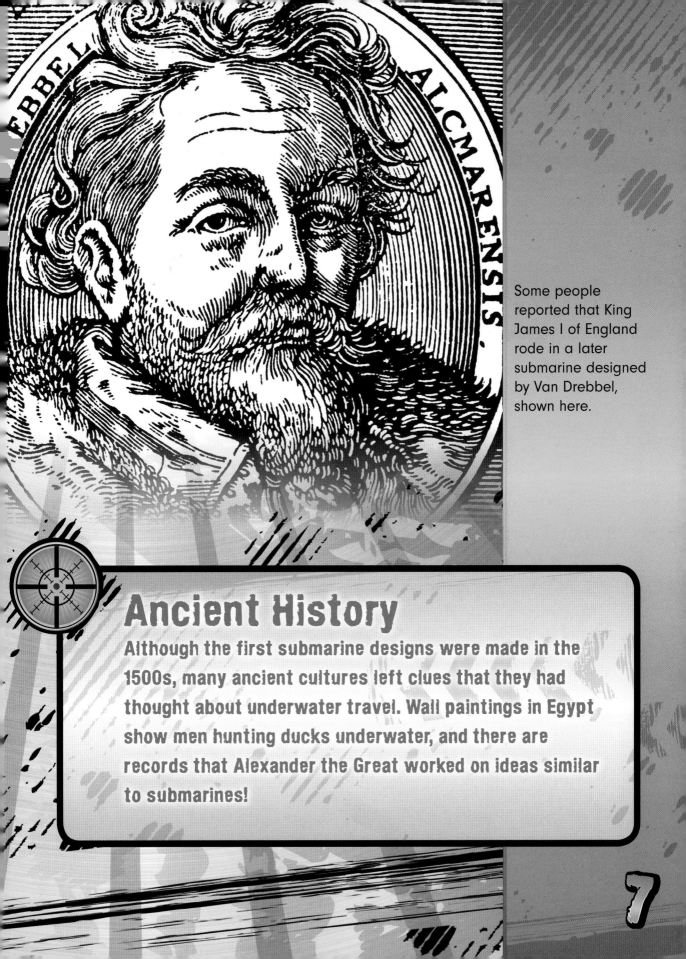

EBBEL   ALCMARENSIS.

Some people reported that King James I of England rode in a later submarine designed by Van Drebbel, shown here.

Ancient History

Although the first submarine designs were made in the 1500s, many ancient cultures left clues that they had thought about underwater travel. Wall paintings in Egypt show men hunting ducks underwater, and there are records that Alexander the Great worked on ideas similar to submarines!

7

THE REVOLUTIONARY TURTLE

Many more people created submarine designs in the 1600s and 1700s. The first submarine-like vessel used to attack an enemy was built in 1776 during the American Revolution. David Bushnell, an American who had just graduated from Yale University, designed what he called the Turtle. It was meant to sneak up on British ships in New York Harbor and attach **mines** to them.

Under the leadership of General George Washington, on September 6, 1776, Sergeant Ezra Lee set out in the Turtle to try and sink the British ship HMS *Eagle*. Even though the vessel worked, the attack was unsuccessful.

Scientific Advancement

Between the American Revolution and the American Civil War, advances in technology around the world led to more successful submarine designs. Among these were the *Nautilus*, built in France by Robert Fulton, and a submarine built by Wilhelm Bauer in Russia. Called *Sea Devil* in English, Bauer's submarine made more than 130 dives!

This is a model of the Turtle based on David Bushnell's design.

SUBS IN THE CIVIL WAR

Both the North and the South in the American Civil War tried to build some kind of submarine to attack the other side. The South's attempt, made by inventor Horace Lawson Hunley, sank twice during its **development**, killing the crew inside both times. The sub was raised and, in 1864, attacked and sank a Northern ship in Charleston Harbor, in South Carolina. After the attack, the *Hunley* sank and was lost for 131 years!

The remains of the *Hunley*, shown here, were finally found in 1995.

The North built a submarine in 1862 called the *Alligator*. It was meant to attack enemy ships in the James River near Richmond, Virginia. But the *Alligator* sank at sea while a boat was towing it.

The *Hunley* was the first submarine to successfully sink a ship in battle.

What's in a Name?

The US Navy used to name submarines after fish or famous figures in American history. Now, the navy names submarines after either a city, state, famous American, or earlier submarine. The *Hunley* was named for its inventor, who died in its second test run.

TURN OF THE CENTURY

The first modern submarine was designed by an Irish-American teacher named John Holland. He powered it with an engine much like today's car engines and sold it to the US Navy in 1900.

A submarine crew stands on the deck of the *Holland* at the US Naval Academy around 1901.

Named the USS *Holland*, it could travel at speeds up to 8 miles (13 km) per hour and carry three torpedoes to attack enemy ships. It had one major flaw, though. When it was underwater, there was no way for the USS *Holland* to see! This was fixed when Simon Lake invented the omniscope, which used a system of mirrors and lenses to let the crew in submarines see above the water.

Days Go By

The USS *Holland* used rechargeable batteries that allowed it to stay underwater for a few hours at a time. This was a large improvement over other submarines of the time. Modern nuclear-powered submarines can stay underwater for months at a time without coming back up to the surface!

THE SUBMARINES OF WWI

Although the United States didn't join World War I until 1917, the British and Germans were fighting with submarines as early as 1914. While the British navy had many more submarines, with 74 in service in 1914, the German "U-boats" were more technologically advanced. They had better engines, **periscopes**, ways to hear underwater, and stronger weapons.

By the time the war ended in November 1918, Germany had built more than 400 submarines. While the Allies sank more than 150 of these, the German U-boats sank more than 4,000 ships and almost won the war with their underwater fighting.

As submarines became more advanced, so did the technology needed to find and fight them.

The Germans practiced "unrestricted submarine warfare," meaning they were using U-boats like this one to attack any ships that came near without warning.

Paying at the Pump

In 1912, the US Navy replaced all the older gasoline engines in its submarines with engines that ran on a fuel called diesel. These were more efficient and safer for two reasons—they didn't need a spark to be lit, reducing fire risk, and they made less poisonous fumes.

THE SUBMARINES OF WWII

During World War II, submarines became more important than they had ever been in the past. The Germans continued to build U-boats as they had during World War I. They tried to use the subs to stop supplies from being sent between the Allies. Using new antisubmarine weapons, British and American forces were able to destroy many of the German U-boats.

While the Allies were fighting Germany in Europe, the United States used its fleet of submarines to fight Japan in the Pacific. Although there weren't that many of them, American submarines sank more than half of all the Japanese ships that were destroyed in World War II.

Radar and Sonar

Among the most important advances in technology for submarines during World War II were the development of radar and sonar for submarine use. Radar uses radio waves to determine where something is and was used to find German U-boats that had surfaced. Sonar uses sound to find things underwater.

This picture shows a radar plot, which is the chart used to show radar's findings.

Antisubmarine weapons included explosives called depth charges, which can be dropped into the water from above.

17

THE COLD WAR AND NUCLEAR SUBS

During the Cold War, the Soviet Union had an advantage in the amount of people and resources it had. But the United States had much more advanced technology. Submarines at this time were used more for **reconnaissance** than fighting. This was made possible by the use of nuclear technology.

The first nuclear submarine, developed by a US Navy scientist named Hyman Rickover, went to sea in 1954. It could stay underwater for much longer than any earlier submarine. Nuclear submarines allowed the United States and the Soviet Union to carry out missions in secret and spy on each other.

How Does the Nuclear Sub Work?

Nuclear subs are powered by nuclear reactors. These reactors contain a **radioactive** metal called uranium. When uranium atoms are split, they release heat. That heat is collected and used to boil water, which creates steam. That steam turns the submarine's engines and gives them power. The amount of fuel on modern submarines will last for more than 30 years!

The United States' first nuclear submarine was called the USS *Nautilus* after the submersible in Jules Verne's book *20,000 Leagues Under the Sea.*

TYPES OF SUBMARINES

Today, the US Navy uses three main kinds of nuclear submarines—attack submarines, guided-**missile** submarines, and ballistic missile submarines.

Attack submarines find and sink enemy ships and submarines. They can launch underwater missiles called torpedoes or release mines into the water. Both attack submarines and guided-missile submarines may carry short-range missiles and support special forces operations. They take part in reconnaissance missions, too.

Ballistic missile submarines, also known as "boomers," carry long-range missiles, including nuclear weapons. These subs keep the location of US nuclear weapons a secret from enemies. If needed, boomers allow for these weapons to be launched accurately without detection.

Submarines can launch huge missiles, such as this D-5 missile called a Trident.

Nuclear Deterrent

The main purpose of ballistic missile submarines isn't to use nuclear weapons on US enemies, but to deter, or stop, other countries from using nuclear weapons on the United States. Each US Navy ballistic missile submarine can hold 24 ballistic missiles, and each missile holds several nuclear bombs called warheads.

SUBMARINE MISSIONS

Each submarine in the US Navy takes part in important missions. Some of these include sea control, or when a submarine doesn't let enemy forces into parts of the ocean. Antisubmarine warfare is finding and fighting other submarines, and antisurface warfare is finding and fighting ships.

There are many missions that don't involve fighting. Strategic deterrence is stopping enemies from attacking by warning them of a counterattack. Subs drop special operations forces to secret locations to fight on land and also transport important people or supplies from one place to another in secret.

What Else Can They Do?

Submarines scout locations and listen in on enemy communications. They also have cruise missile strike capability. That means missiles can be launched from the submarine to targets on land. One of submarines' most important jobs is the search and rescue of downed pilots or ground forces stuck near water.

Every submarine
mission requires
preparation and
careful planning.

BEING A SUBMARINER

To work on a submarine, first you must join the US Navy. Then, after regular military training, sailors can **volunteer** to work on a submarine. But not everyone who volunteers completes training. First, a sailor must pass certain tests. Then, he must attend schools for special submarine training.

Submarine crews must be able to operate, maintain, and repair everything on one of the most technologically advanced military machines the US military has. Even once they're aboard the sub, crews continue to learn about new technology and sub operations. Crews include electricians, chemists, weapons technicians, navigators, clerks, and even cooks.

This sailor is using a realistic training program to refresh his knowledge of driving a submarine.

Submariners must be able to work quickly and calmly in dangerous situations. This sailor is working to fix a problem that could lead to flooding.

A Picky Bunch

Only certain people are allowed to work on submarines. If someone is claustrophobic, or afraid of small places, the navy doesn't allow them to be on a submarine crew. The US Navy wants to make sure that everyone on the crew will be safe and healthy.

MODERN SUBMERSIBLES

The history of submersibles is closely tied to that of submarines. Manned submersibles carry a crew and have life support systems, such as oxygen and heat control. Unmanned submersibles may be remotely operated **vehicles** (ROVs), which means they're controlled from land or aboard a ship and are connected to a power source. Autonomous underwater vehicles (AUVs) aren't connected to any power source or other vehicle. They carry out missions programmed into their computer systems.

All submersibles have lights or video cameras. Many are built with mechanical arms to collect samples and complete tasks outside the vessel.

Navy SEALs and divers take part in special training to ready them for missions using submersibles.

The US military uses submersibles for reconnaissance and rescue, in addition to other missions. Sometimes these are called "minisubs" because they move people and supplies like submarines do.

SDV

The Navy SEALs delivery vehicle (SDV) is a submersible that brings Navy SEALs to mission locations in secret. The US military started developing these submersibles during World War II, and SEALs began to use a modern model in 1975. SDVs are called "flooded vessels"—the SEALs travel outside the SDV using SCUBA gear!

THE FUTURE UNDERWATER

The United States and other countries around the world continue to build better, more effective submarines and submersibles. There are more than 40 countries that have submarines. Countries with nuclear submarines in their fleet include Great Britain, France, China, and Russia.

US submarines are always active in waters around the world. In the future, submarines will be smaller, able to operate without help, and controlled by the navy from afar, rather than by people inside of them. Submersibles that can operate both on and below the water are already being made!

Famous Submersibles

The *Aluminaut* was a submersible that could carry a crew of six people more than 15,000 feet (4,572 m) under the surface. It was retired in 1970. The *Alvin*, which was built in the 1960s, was used with other submersibles to raise parts of the *Titanic* from the ocean floor.

Submarines are an important part of modern warfare.

29

GLOSSARY

atom: one of the smallest bits of matter

design: to create the pattern or shape of something. Also, the pattern or shape of something.

development: the act of creating over time

maneuver: a planned and skillful movement

mine: an explosive often buried in the ground or hidden underwater

missile: a rocket used to strike something at a distance

mission: a task or job a group must perform

periscope: an instrument on submarines that uses mirrors and lenses to see above water

radioactive: a material that gives off energy when its atoms change

reconnaissance: the exploration of a place to collect information

submerge: to put or sink below the surface of water

technology: the practical application of specialized knowledge

vehicle: an object used for carrying or transporting people or goods, such as a car, truck, or airplane

volunteer: to offer service without being asked

FOR MORE INFORMATION

Books

Abramson, Andra Serlin. *Submarines Up Close*. New York, NY: Sterling, 2007.

Doeden, Matt. *Submarines*. Minneapolis, MN: Lerner Publications Company, 2006.

Lock, Deborah. *Submarines and Submersibles*. New York, NY: DK Publishing, 2007.

Websites

How Submarines Work
science.howstuffworks.com/transport/engines-equipment/submarine.htm
Read a detailed explanation about how a submarine works.

US Navy Homepage
www.navy.mil
Check out the US Navy website with information about submarines and submersibles.

INDEX